21st
Century
Skills Library

COOL CAREERS

CARPENTER

SUSAN HINDMAN

Published in the United States of America by
Cherry Lake Publishing, Ann Arbor, Michigan
www.cherrylakepublishing.com

Content Adviser
Charlie Mundy, Carpentry Instructor, Southwestern Community College,
Osceola, Iowa

Credits
Photos: Cover and page 1, ©James Peragine/Shutterstock, Inc.; page 4,
©iStockphoto.com/GeorgePeters; page 7, ©cappi thompson/Shutterstock, Inc.;
page 8, ©Vivid Pixels/Shutterstock, Inc.; page 11, ©Christina Richards/
Shutterstock, Inc.; page 12, ©Melissa Dockstader/Shutterstock, Inc.; page 14,
©Brandon Bourdages/Shutterstock, Inc.; page 16, ©nateperro/Shutterstock, Inc.;
pages 18 and 28, ©Jim West/Alamy; page 20, ©iStockphoto.com/RichVintage;
page 23, ©Stephen Coburn/Shutterstock, Inc.; page 24, ©r.martens/Shutterstock,
Inc.; page 26, ©JHDT Stock Images LLC/Shutterstock, Inc.

Library of Congress Cataloging-in-Publication Data
Hindman, Susan.
 Carpenter/by Susan Hindman.
    p. cm.—(Cool careers)
 Includes bibliographical references and index.
 ISBN-13: 978-1-60279-935-6 (lib. bdg.)
 ISBN-10: 1-60279-935-0 (lib. bdg.)
 1. Carpentry—Vocational guidance—Juvenile literature.
 2. Carpenters—Juvenile literature. I. Title. II. Series.
 TH5608.7.H56 2010
 694.023—dc22   2010000694

Cherry Lake Publishing would like to acknowledge
the work of The Partnership for 21st Century Skills.
Please visit www.21stcenturyskills.org for more information.

Printed in the United States of America
Corporate Graphics Inc.
July 2010
CLFA07

TABLE OF CONTENTS

CHAPTER ONE
STARTING THE JOB 4

CHAPTER TWO
WHAT CARPENTERS DO 12

CHAPTER THREE
BECOMING A CARPENTER 18

CHAPTER FOUR
**TECHNOLOGY LENDS
   A HAND** 24

SOME WELL-KNOWN CARPENTERS 29
GLOSSARY 30
FOR MORE INFORMATION 31
INDEX. .32
ABOUT THE AUTHOR. 32

CARPENTER

CHAPTER ONE
STARTING THE JOB

The carpenter looks over his schedule for the first morning of a kitchen **remodel**. At 8 A.M., he'll meet his helpers at the

It takes a lot of planning and hard work to design and build a custom kitchen.

job site. They will help him move the appliances into another room. Then they will help him remove the counters, cabinets, and wall tiles. The room will be almost empty by the end of the day.

This will be a dusty, dirty day. The carpenter makes sure he has what he needs in his toolbox and tool belt. He loads building materials into his truck. He grabs his jacket and stops to think for a moment. He remembers his grandfather, a carpenter who wore bib overalls to every job. The overalls had loops for holding tools. That was then. The carpenter smiles to himself. He looks down at his own jeans and T-shirt. This is now.

He arrives at the job site and spends some time talking with the homeowner. They carefully go over the work schedule together. The carpenter doesn't want the homeowner to be surprised by anything. The homeowner needs to find a place to cook while the work is being done.

The carpenter and his helpers get to work. The carpenter carefully inspects the room at the end of the day to make sure nothing was overlooked. Then he sweeps the floor and hauls away the old kitchen materials.

The room will see big changes during the next week. The carpenter's daily plans will change, too. Is he putting up drywall? Will he be painting? Is the new floor going in today? Some materials may need to be cut before they are installed.

The carpenter makes sure he brings the right tools to do that. He only brings the materials he needs for that day.

The carpenter has already built cabinets and a five-shelf pantry at his shop. The countertops have been cut to fit the space he measured. He will bring these things from the shop to the job site so they can be installed.

Each day, the carpenter tells the homeowner what will come next. Sometimes he might be ahead of schedule. Other times, he might be a little behind. He makes sure the owner knows exactly how far along the job is.

LEARNING & INNOVATION SKILLS

Ancient Babylonians had to follow the Code of Hammurabi. Some of the code's rules about carpentry were very strict. Rule 229 said that a builder would be put to death if a house he built fell in and killed the owner. If the house killed the homeowner's son, then Rule 230 said that the builder's son was to be put to death. Would you want to be a carpenter if these rules were still being enforced? Why or why not?

Carpenters must take careful measurements.

People remodel kitchens and other rooms for many different reasons. Sometimes they need more cabinet or counter space. Other times, water pipes can leak and cause damage to walls or floors. Often, people just want to give an old room a new look. Carpenters can help them do all this and more.

Carpenters use their knowledge and skills to assist with almost every part of a building's construction.

Carpenters are skilled construction workers. They build, install, and repair structures made from wood and other materials. The structure may be a room or an entire home. That isn't all they do, though. Carpenters construct the buildings, bridges, and highways you see every day. They build everything from the **foundation** to the top.

21ST CENTURY CONTENT

Joinery is the work of cutting and fitting pieces of wood together without using nails or glue. In the 1700s, joinery was a very **specialized** craft. Carpenters assembled wood into structures. Joiners worked on projects with complicated intersections, such as spiral staircases or window shutters. Pieces of wood were notched and fitted together to create what is called a dovetail joint. Construction methods changed over time, though. Carpentry and joinery combined into one business. Joinery is rarely done anymore, and the term *joiner* is no longer used.

Many people think that carpenters only work with wood. Ancient peoples built structures out of stone, brick, and mud. Today's carpenters also work with metals, plastics, and concrete. They also use premade materials such as drywall, plywood, and hardwood flooring.

During the Middle Ages, carpenters specialized in building things such as wooden ships, wheels, or barrels. They often lived in larger towns and traveled to smaller towns when needed.

Before the 1800s, building materials were crafted by hand. Bricks, boards, and even nails were handmade. Then factories began **mass-producing** construction supplies and **prefabricated** materials. This put an end to the construction of completely handmade homes.

LEARNING & INNOVATION SKILLS

Though most construction materials are no longer handmade, some carpenters continue to craft one-of-a-kind items. Would you be willing to pay more for handmade cabinets, furniture, or other items made of wood? Why or why not?

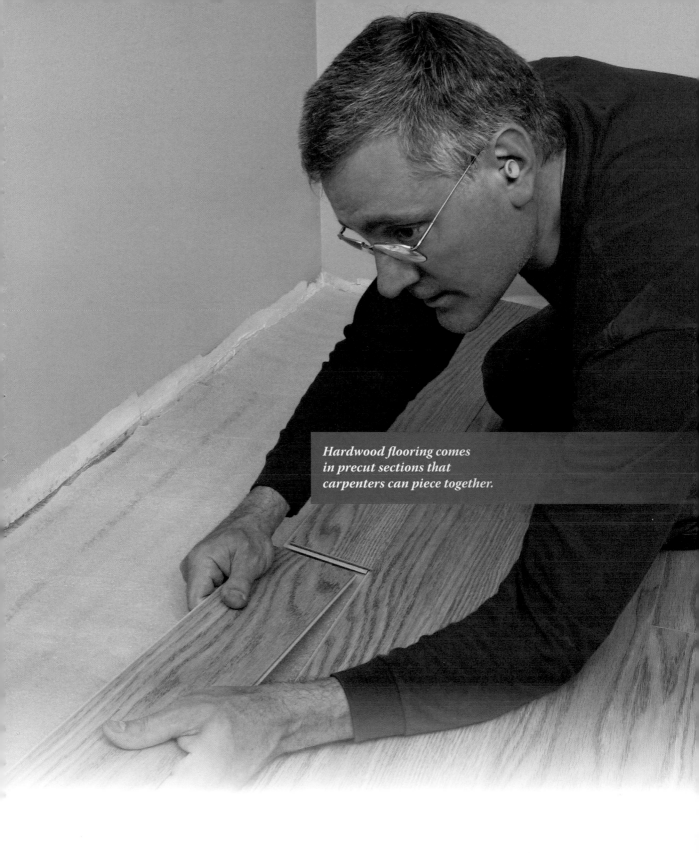

Hardwood flooring comes in precut sections that carpenters can piece together.

CHAPTER TWO
WHAT CARPENTERS DO

Today's carpenters do many different types of work. They build the wood frames for concrete foundations. They put up

Carpenters construct wooden frames that serve as a building's skeleton.

walls, build stairways, and hang windows. They install
countertops and sinks. They even paint walls.

LEARNING & INNOVATION SKILLS

Where would you start if you were remodeling a
bathroom? What would you replace? What would
improve the room? A lot of planning goes into
a remodeling job. "From there, it's like putting
together a puzzle," says Dave Bush. Bush is a
third-generation master carpenter. He has worked
in the industry for 30 years. He owns PDQ Home
Improvements in Palmer Lake, Colorado. "You
think, lay it out, and do calculations with paper
and pencil. You have the tools set up so you
can function throughout the project. You install
everything in the right order. No matter what you
do, you have to have a plan."

Some carpenters start out as apprentices. Apprentices
train with master carpenters. They become journeymen when
they are more experienced. In time, journeymen become
master carpenters.

Some carpenters may work alone in a home. Others work as part of a team at a construction site. They may specialize in certain tasks.

Rough carpenters are also called framers. They build the wooden framework for buildings. They also build concrete forms, **scaffolds**, and bridge supports.

Finish carpenters are also called trim carpenters. They install baseboards, doors, and windows. They also work with paneling, stairways, and trim. These are the things people will see when the building is complete.

Scaffolds help carpenters and other construction experts work on tall buildings.

Cabinet and furniture makers are more specialized carpenters. They can do very detailed wood work. They don't usually work on the construction of buildings. Most of their time is spent working at their shops.

Carpenters usually wear long pants, T-shirts, and work boots. They don't worry about getting their clothes dirty. They are careful to wear clothes that aren't too loose. Loose clothes can get in the way or get caught in power tools. Most carpenters don't wear rings or watches.

Carpenters wear boots with steel toes and heavy soles to protect their feet from sharp or heavy objects. They wear safety glasses or goggles to protect their eyes. Earplugs or earmuffs help protect their hearing. They often wear breathing masks if they are going to be around chemicals. Hard hats protect their heads at construction sites.

Carpenters measure, cut, and piece together building materials. They use saws, drills, and many other tools. Rulers and squares help them measure materials. Plumb lines and levels help make sure materials are **aligned**. Stud finders tell carpenters where the wood supports are inside a wall. Ripping bars and crowbars help them pry materials apart. Carpenters also use power tools such as sanders, table saws, and nail guns. These tools save time and help make work easier. Carpenters keep their tools in good working order. They may carry sharpening stones to keep their tools from getting dull.

Glue, nails, and tape hold materials together. Wood pencils allow carpenters to mark their measurements on the materials. Chalk boxes are used to mark straight lines.

Stone Age people used stone axes to shape wood. They built animal traps, boats, and shelters. Egyptians used copper woodworking tools as early as 4000 BCE. By 2000 BCE, woodworking tools were made from bronze. Roman carpenters

Modern tools help carpenters cut and shape pieces of wood.

between 400 BCE and 500 CE used tools such as rasps, awls, and planes. Rasps look like files. They are used for shaping building material. Awls are like spikes. They can punch holes or mark wood. Planes are blades that make surfaces smooth. Many of these tools are still used today. Modern versions are made of different materials.

21ST CENTURY CONTENT

Carpenters usually need to get building permits before starting jobs. This is how cities make sure their building codes are followed. These codes are based on the International Residential Code. Codes are a little different in each city. For example, California has many earthquakes. Colorado gets heavy snow. The Midwest has tornados. Building codes in those places deal with these weather problems.

CHAPTER THREE
BECOMING A CARPENTER

Carpenters have to be in good physical shape. They spend a lot of time climbing, bending, and kneeling.

Carpenters must be able to kneel, climb, bend, and lift heavy materials.

They lift heavy materials and hold them in uncomfortable positions. They work with sharp tools and noisy machines. They may work high in the air while standing on narrow ledges. Sometimes they have to work outdoors in bad weather. They often work very long hours during the summer.

Carpenters like working with their hands. They have to be willing to work indoors and outdoors. Knowing how to properly use machines and tools is a must. Carpenters can picture what a room is going to look like long before it is done. Do you think you have what it takes to be a carpenter?

 LIFE & CAREER SKILLS

Some carpenters begin developing their skills at an early age. Master carpenter Dave Bush showed an interest in carpentry when he was very young. "I took things apart at an early age," said Bush. "I was always playing with Erector Sets and Lincoln Logs." His family was also an inspiration. Bush's grandfather was a "really good carpenter" and his uncle was a finish carpenter. His father was also skilled at carpentry. "This was given to me. They passed it on to me," he believes.

To be a carpenter, you need a good education. Math skills are very important. Carpenters need to understand angles, **dimensions**, and fractions so they can measure building materials. They also have to estimate how much material they need for a job. They have to tell homeowners how long jobs will take and how much they will cost.

The ability to read blueprints and other design drawings is a necessary skill for every carpenter.

Future carpenters don't just study math in high school. They also take classes in English, physics, and **industrial arts**. This helps them begin learning how to follow directions on **blueprints** and design drawings.

Trade schools and community colleges offer classes for students to learn carpentry skills. Future carpenters should also learn technical writing and graphics programs. Classes in industrial safety are also a good idea. Schools and employers offer apprenticeship programs. These programs are a great way for future carpenters to get hands-on job experience.

A carpenter's job experience can affect how much money he makes. Most carpenters make between $14.00 and $25.00 per hour. Experienced carpenters can make more than $33.00 per hour. The amount of money carpenters make also depends on the demand for new construction. Sometimes, there might not be much work available. Other times, they can make extra money by working overtime.

Some carpenters may go on to become contractors. Contractors run construction businesses. They hire people to help them with big jobs.

Carpenters need to learn about different kinds of building materials. Each material is best used for different things. The same is true of tools. Carpenters also need to know how to repair and take care of their power tools.

Finally, carpenters need people skills. They need to convince homeowners that they are right for the job. Carpenters also work with other **subcontractors** such as plumbers and electricians. Carpenters with better training and more skills have an easier time finding work.

21ST CENTURY CONTENT

The first carpenters' guilds were started around the 12th century. These guilds were designed to protect workers' rights. They were early versions of unions. One of the first unions was The Carpenters' Company of the City and County of Philadelphia. It was formed in 1724. It published a secret rule book for its members in 1786. The book set prices for the different jobs that carpenters did. In 1881, a national union called the United Brotherhood of Carpenters and Joiners (UBC) was formed. In 2009, the UBC had more than half a million members. It offers training at centers across the country.

Carpenters need to be able to get along with homeowners and other construction workers.

CHAPTER FOUR
TECHNOLOGY LENS A HAND

T here are more than 1 million carpenters working in the United States. Most work for contractors. They help build

Some carpenters have workshops filled with tools to help them shape wood for building furniture.

and repair buildings. Others work for stores, schools, and the government. About one-third of them have their own businesses.

New tools and materials have changed the way carpenters do their jobs. For example, wall panels, roof assemblies, and stairs are not usually built on the job site. Instead, they are made in factories. Carpenters use machines to lift the prebuilt pieces into place.

LEARNING & INNOVATION SKILLS

Ladders and scaffolding allow carpenters to work in high places. They need the help of machines to work on very tall buildings, though. So how did workers in ancient Egypt move heavy stones to the top of the pyramids? The Great Pyramid is 481 feet (147 meters) tall. That's as tall as a 48-story building!

Scholars aren't sure how these pyramids were built. One theory is that the ancient Egyptians built ramps out of mud bricks and plaster. These ramps wrapped around the outside of the pyramid. The stones would be moved along the ramps. Ramps may also have been used inside the pyramids. Can you think of any other ways the pyramids might have been built?

Modern carpenters also use computer technology. Computer-aided design (CAD) software helps them create blueprints and models of their projects. These can easily be resized and rotated on the computer. Accounting software helps carpenters run their businesses. Other programs help them figure out costs for jobs. Many carpenters

Computer software is becoming more and more important to carpenters and others who work in construction.

today have their own Web sites. This can help them get
more jobs. Employment for carpenters is expected to
continue growing.

21ST CENTURY CONTENT

Colonial Williamsburg in Virginia is home to many
examples of 18th century carpentry. Eighty-eight
of the town's buildings are original. Hundreds
more have been rebuilt by skilled carpenters.
These carpenters study the original building
manuals and documents of the era. No modern
machinery is used.

Researchers discovered that there were
three groups of carpenters in colonial Virginia.
Clapboard carpenters built homes in the
countryside and other simple projects. African
American carpenters were often slaves who had
been trained. They usually had about the same
skills as the clapboard carpenter. Accomplished
carpenters worked on the most difficult projects.

Carpenters help shape communities as they grow and change. They help create our homes, businesses, and other buildings. They also help update the things we already have by rebuilding and remodeling them. Their hard work ensures that our buildings are sturdy and pleasing to look at, both inside and out. With a little hard work, you can become a carpenter. Then you can leave your mark on the places where we live, work, and spend our free time.

Why not look for opportunities to practice using tools? Maybe you will be a carpenter someday!

SOME WELL-KNOWN CARPENTERS

Norm Abram (1950–) is a master carpenter who is best known for his PBS television show *This Old House.* The show is about remodeling and improving old houses. It is still on the air. Abram also hosted *The New Yankee Workshop.* This show ended in 2009 after 20 years on the air. He has published 8 books about carpentry. In 2009, the American Academy of Ophthalmology awarded him the first EyeSmart Distinguished Service Award. This award is given to people who work to promote eye safety.

David J. Marks (?–) is an award-winning woodworker. He hosted the television show *Wood Works.* The show featured step-by-step instructions for building furniture.

Peter J. "P. J." McGuire (1852–1906) was one of the founders of the United Brotherhood of Carpenters and Joiners in 1881. He spoke about working conditions and the need for a national union of carpenters. His work led to the 8-hour workday and higher pay for workers. Some records show that he created Labor Day, which was first celebrated in 1882.

Samuel McIntire (1757–1811) was a master carpenter, woodcarver, and architect in New England during the late 18th century. His buildings in Salem, Massachusetts, were decorated with detailed woodwork. He competed for the job of designing the United States Capitol in 1792. There is an historic area named after him in Salem.

Benjamin Powell (1730–1791) has been called Colonial Williamsburg's most successful carpenter. He worked on many of the town's public buildings. He ran a general contracting business from his home. Visitors to Colonial Williamsburg can still see the original Benjamin Powell House.

GLOSSARY

aligned (uh-LINED) in a straight line

blueprints (BLU-printss) detailed plans for a structure

dimensions (dih-MEN-shuhnz) the measurements of something in length, width, and often height or depth

foundation (foun-DAY-shuhn) the supportive bottom or base of a structure

industrial arts (inn-DUSS-tree-uhl ARTSS) a class in which students learn to use tools and machines to build and repair things

mass-producing (MASS pruh-DOOS-eng) manufacturing large numbers of goods at one time

prefabricated (pree-FAB-rih-kay-tid) made ahead of time

remodel (ree-MAH-duhl) rebuild

scaffolds (SKAF-fuhldz) frameworks put up to support workers while they are building, repairing, or painting something

specialized (SPESH-uh-lized) focused on one area of work

subcontractors (sub-KON-trak-turz) companies that are paid to take on some of the main contractor's job

FOR MORE INFORMATION

BOOKS

Horn, Geoffrey M. *Construction Worker*. Pleasantville, NY: Gareth Stevens Publishing, 2009.

Kelsey, John. *Woodworking*. East Petersburg, PA: Fox Chapel Publishing, 2008.

Macken, JoAnn Early. *Building a House*. Mankato, MN: Capstone Press, 2009.

WEB SITES

Bureau of Labor Statistics—Occupational Outlook Handbook, 2010–11 Edition: Carpenters
www.bls.gov/oco/ocos202.htm
Read about the training carpenters need, how much they earn, and other information about the profession.

This Old House—Family Projects
www.thisoldhouse.com/toh/info/0,,20168465,00.html
Watch videos and see step-by-step pictures of simple projects such as "How to Build a Lemonade Stand," "How to Build a Bird Feeder, "Building a Fort," and many more.

INDEX

apprentices, 13, 21
awls, 17

blueprints, 21, 26
building codes, 6, 17
building materials, 5, 6, 9, 10, 15, 16, 17, 19, 20, 21, 25
building permits, 17
Bush, Dave, 13, 19

cabinet makers, 6, 15
clapboard carpenters, 27
clothing, 5, 15
Colonial Williamsburg, 27, 29
community colleges, 21
contractors, 21, 24
costs, 20, 26

demand, 21
design drawings, 21, 26
dovetail joints, 9

earthquakes, 17
education, 20–21, 22
Egyptians, 16, 25
estimates, 20

factories, 10, 25
finish carpenters, 14, 19
foundations, 9, 12
furniture makers, 15

guilds, 22

joinery, 9
journeymen, 13

master carpenters, 13, 19, 29
measurements, 6, 15, 16, 20
Middle Ages, 10

people skills, 22
physical shape, 18–19
planes, 16–17

power tools, 15, 21
pyramids, 25

rasps, 16–17
remodeling, 4–6, 8, 13, 28, 29
Romans, 16–17
rough carpenters, 14

safety, 15, 21, 29
salaries, 21
slavery, 27
Stone Age, 16
subcontractors, 22

technology, 26–27
tools, 5–6, 13, 15–17, 19, 21, 25
trade schools, 21

unions, 22, 29

weather, 17, 19
Web sites, 26–27
work schedules, 4–5, 6

ABOUT THE AUTHOR

Susan Hindman has had a freelance editing and writing business in Colorado Springs, Colorado, since 1997. Before that, she worked in newspapers as a copyeditor, page designer, and writer. She has two college-age daughters. Susan has hired carpenters through the years to work on her 43-year-old home and enjoys watching all the changes.